ANTHOLOGY OF POETRY BY YOUNG AMERICANS®

2006 EDITION
VOLUME XXII

Published by Anthology of Poetry, Inc.

©*Anthology of Poetry by Young Americans*®
2006 Edition
Volume XXII

All Rights Reserved©

Printed in the United States of America

To submit poems
for consideration in the year 2007 edition of the
Anthology of Poetry by Young Americans®,
go to: anthologyofpoetry.com or

>Anthology of Poetry, Inc.
>PO Box 698
>Asheboro, NC 27204-0698

Authors responsible
for originality of poems submitted.

Anthology of Poetry, Inc.
307 East Salisbury • P.O. Box 698
Asheboro, NC   27204-0698

Paperback ISBN: 1-883931-60-6
Hardback ISBN: 1-883931-59-2

Anthology of Poetry by Young Americans®
is a registered trademark of
Anthology of Poetry, Inc.

For the past seventeen years, the *Anthology of Poetry by Young Americans®* has presented the written art of some of the most creative students across the country. Unlike a painted canvas that is delivered to its audience in the final form, the written word is an art of rhythmic emergence, engaging the reader as the story develops with a cadence shared by both the writer and the audience. The reader is given the gift of the developing art by the writer who entrusts all in the audience with the uniquely individual responsibility of painting their own canvases as they go. The written word is a shared art, handed off by the writer for the audience to finish.

Over the years, at Anthology of Poetry, we have received countless letters of appreciation from teachers, students, parents, and grandparents. For these we are grateful, and humbled, just as we have been by the submissions of poetry by students from the thousands of schools that participate each year. And just as the written word is shared art between the writer and the reader, the thanks and congratulations must be shared with the students who have created their art, with the readers they will never meet, and with their loving family members who have encouraged these young writers to express themselves through their poetry.

Once again we are proud to present to you, the reader, the other half of the emerging process of storytelling, the *Anthology of Poetry by Young Americans®* for 2006. You have arrived here ready to participate in the art of the written word, so open your senses and be ready to paint your canvases in the vivid colors, textures, and rhythms of the stories presented to us by these creative and brave young artists.

The Editors

THE PAST

Tomorrow will be the start
The start of something new
The old is in the past
The new is in the future
The future holds something
Something I do not know
The past is something old
But the past is what I know
These memories have been in the making
For years
Years of my life I've done everything the same
But that's all about to change
Every day is something different
Something new, good or bad
The future is to not knowing
Not knowing what is coming is to being afraid
Being afraid of letting go
Letting go of the past
Your friends become the strangers
The strangers become your friends
Now all you can see are those days passing you by
But the one thing that lasts
Are the memories in the past.

Michele Nicole Griffith
Age: 14

DIFFERENT COLORS!

Some people have blonde hair
Some have brown.
Some even have black.
Not me. I
I am a redhead.
No Lie!
When a little kid
comes up to me
and asks,
"Why
do you
have
orange hair?"
I say, "It's not orange it's red."
It's not that I'm sad about it.
I'm very proud.
Proud
because I have
one-of-a-kind hair!
No Lie!
That's what I love
about me!

Brittany Karlheim
Age: 13

MY GRANDMA

My grandma is as tall as me,
and that is only five feet three.
People say she is short and kind,
I believe they have the right picture in their minds.
She is a grandma who is nice,
and the kind who adds extra cheese to your cheesy rice.
My grandma has blonde hair,
which you can see almost anywhere.
She bakes pizzas, cookies, and pies,
and even spaghetti with your favorite brand of bow ties.
She'll take us to the playground or even the park,
she will let us stay up way past dark.
She will give you that extra scoop,
of ice cream before a supper of soup.
She will take you places like a candy shop,
just to buy a single lollipop.
She has many more great things about her
she will never become a blur.
This poem could go on forever,
but then it would cease never.

Luke Gindlesperger
Age: 11

AND THE WINNER IS . . .

The Reading Competition this fall
Will be at Roosevelt High School.
The main point of this competition
Is that reading is cool!

On the list there are forty-two books.
I have read twenty-four.
My favorite book is THE CHRISTMAS SPURS.
My least favorite is EVVY'S CIVIL WAR.

The sixth grade team is called the Blue Eagles.
We have two readers on just about every book.
We started reading at the beginning of the summer.
That's how long it took!

We've worked truly very hard this year.
I really hope we win best overall.
But, of course I can settle
For a blue ribbon hanging in the hall.

> Lisa Vatavuk
> Age: 11

RAIN

There's something soothing about the rain.
BIG or small droplets collected
Somewhere,
     Anywhere,
          EVERYWHERE.

    Dr
     ip
       pi
          ng on the roof
Sounding like paint S p L a T t E r I n G on a canvas.
This sound fills my heart.

          Karlee Lyn Ertter
              Age: 14

WORDS

Words! You see them everywhere
Especially in Delaware
Words can rhyme
They sometimes sound like a dime
Words can be long
Words can be short
It doesn't matter how you spell them
They always mean the same
Words can be happy
Words can be sad
Words can be fun
Words can be boring
Words can be sharp
Words can be dull
It doesn't matter how you spell them
They always mean the same
Words can be cool
You spell them in school
You use them at work
You use them at play
You learn them at two
You slur them at ninety-two
Words! You see them everywhere
Especially in Delaware
It doesn't matter how you spell them
They always mean the same

James Palmer
Age: 12

Look over yonder she is here
The way she walks
She is coming I should go
Wait stop why run from thee
I do not understand

Do you hate thee
No I dare not I
I was getting a gift
But I dare not say
For you will have to wait another day

Here she is here are you?
Shhh quiet I am ready
There she is my bride to be
My lady will you marry thee
For all eternity I plea

Tyler Campbell
Age: 12

ON HALLOWEEN NIGHT

You can hear the whistling air on Halloween night,
It scares you quite a bit shuddering with fright.

You feel a tap and turn around,
There is a skeleton on the ground.

Suddenly you wake up and loudly scream,
And realize . . . it was just a dream

Natasha Sharma
Age: 10

THE RIVER'S CURRENT

The river's current was running fast!
Swift like pouring milk in a glass!
As fast as a fish can swim downstream!
Fast as the wind blows leaves from a tree!

Noah Noel

THY KNIGHT'S LOVE

What doth I hear
a battle out yonder
in the grassy fields
I await for my knight
to arrive and rescue me

As I sit here in thy
great castle my grief
overcomes me knowing
that my knight may not
have survived through
thy battle

'Tis the sound of his
horn do I hear arise
Over the great green hill
thy heart beats furiously
as I see his armour come upon me

As he approaches through
thy gate I see the twinkle
in his beautiful blue eyes
and know that thy great
castle is safe at last

Dylana Wartluft
Age: 11

KNIGHT PASSING THROUGH

Thou knight passed through the village
a peaceful little place to be
people's heads begin turning and looking
sad for the knight, thou battle he must go
family he must leave

Shining silvery horse
the knight is sitting upon
he passes merchants and women
it makes him lonely of his own village
he is missing his loved ones

Sitting upon his horse
he thinks of writing poetry
and misses his wife and children
soon he is through the town, heading toward the battle
a tear drops down his cheek

Maria Heintzinger
Age: 11

The stars dance in the moonlight.
The moon whispers to the sun
"Remember to wake up the people."
Then dawn swoops down around the corner,
bringing night, the moon and the stars back again.

Rylee Franz
Age: 11

ELEPHANT TRIP

To Istanbul I went,
Riding on an elephant.
We passed a group of boys,
And they were making lots of noise.
My elephant thought they were frightening,
So, he ran away as fast as lightning!

Kate Kuczynski
Age: 11

MY FOUR-HEADED BUTTERFLY FRIEND

One day when I was flying,
On my new Quad Drooble Oople Shining.
I saw a four-headed butterfly,
Who was soaring through the sky.
So I asked him where he was going,
And he said, oh I am just roaming.
Then I asked where he was from,
He replied the land of Bubblegum.
He told me to follow him,
So then we were off on a whim.
When we got there I was amazed,
Boy-o-boy I was amazed.
So he became my friend,
The four-headed butterfly, Ken.

Michelle Watson
Age: 12

ANGELENE RAPONE

Angelene
Brunette, fun, athletic, tall
Sister of Christina
One who loves my dog, my family, and Mexico
Who feels excited when I have a basketball game,
   happy to see my friends, and sad if I get a bad grade
Who needs time to myself, supper every day,
   and TV before bed
Who gives my old clothes to the poor, love to my family,
   and help to my sister
Who fears terrorists, spiders, and death
Who would like to go to Italy,
   get a convertible when I'm sixteen,
   and play in the WNBA
Resident of Pennsylvania
Rapone

                                        Angelene Rapone
                                              Age: 11

Michelle
Tall, shy, friendly, energetic
Daughter of Mary and Mike
One who loves skateboarding, my family and music
Who feels shy meeting new people,
   excited to go see my dad
   and disappointed when I go home
Who needs to practice the guitar, study, and run every day
Who gives my mom help, the pets food,
   and money to the church
Who fears of clowns, car crashes,
   and my nightmares coming true
Who likes to play the guitar in a band, go to a skate park,
   and meet Mest
Resident of Pennsylvania
Pruchnic

                                      Michelle Pruchnic
                                                Age: 11

VETERAN

V olunteered to protect the U.S.
E qual pride
T ook risks
E veryone is thankful
R emembered forever
A soldier that sacrificed their life
N ever gave up to give us freedom

Joseph Ladesic
Age: 11

THE REAL ME

I'm really a rock star every day,
I'll show my skills in every way.
Yesterday, I went to China and back,
To perform my funny but wonderful act.
Tomorrow, I will go to Peru,
To sing and dance at the zoo!
So now you know a little more about me,
I'm a rock star can't you see!?

Jennifer Jopek
Age: 12

Brittany
Nice, tall, happy, energetic
Sister of Cody and Ricky
One who loves my family, animals, and shopping
Who feels happy to spend time with family,
   glad to have pets and to travel
Who needs sleep every night, water every day,
   and time to feed pets
Who gives love to family, food to pets, help to my brother
Who fears, spiders, bees, and fire
Who would like to go to Florida, go to Texas,
   and win one million dollars.
Resident of Pennsylvania
Jones

                                               Brittany Jones
                                                 Age: 11

CHRISTIAN RENA

Christian
Nice, unpredictable, giving, friendly.
Brother of Maynard.
One who loves ice cream, my mom, and swimming.
Excited to draw, shy when meeting new people,
   tired when running up stairs.
One who needs to drink a lot, more friends, more money.
One who gives care for my baby cousin, a good friend,
   laughter to others.
One who fears big moving statues, snakes that bite,
   big poisonous spiders.
Who would like to fly, go to Mexico, be an artist.
Resident of Pennsylvania
Rena

                                           Chris-Ian Rena
                                              Age: 11

MATT A. CILLI

Matt
Tall, athletic, energetic, fun
Brother of Marc
One who loves my family, Duke, and the Eagles
Who feels happy to spend time playing sports,
   to start fall ball, to get home from school every day
Who needs food, water, and shelter every day,
   to get sleep, and to feed my cats
Who fears scorpions, Bigfoot, and big dogs.
Who would like to visit Canada, eat pizza every day,
   and play sports
Resident of Pennsylvania
Cilli

Matthew A. Cilli
Age: 12

JOE SEABURN

Athletic, tall, fast, organized
Brother of Samantha
One who loves family, football, and food
Who feels happy it's football season, sad school is back,
 and mad I can't sleep in
Who needs football, food, and sleep
Who gives hugs to my family, gives food and pets
 to my dog
Who fears to fail in anything, to get killed,
 not to make it to the NFL
Who would like to go to Niagara Falls, sleep all day
 and play football
Resident of Pennsylvania.

Joe Seaburn
Age: 11

APPLE CIDER

Don't be mean be nicer,
And I'll give you apple cider.
Hey let's go look at a spider,
On top of a big fat glider.
Then let's get some wheat,
And then we all can eat.

Joseph E. Brown
Age: 12

VETERANS DAY

H elping others
E veryone respects you
R ed, white, and blue
O h beautiful for spacious skies

David Stoops
Age: 12

I REMEMBER

I remember how his hair was a grayish brown,
And how he used to catch me before I hit the ground.

I remember how he knew almost everyone,
And how he used to make something boring really fun.

I remember his clothes would never really match,
And how he used to take me to the pumpkin patch.

He always wore sunglasses and a certain hat too,
I really really miss him, yes I truly do.

I remember that night we were sad and lost our pride,
But wouldn't you have felt that way if you found
  your dad had died?

                                        Leah Cozza
                                         Age: 11

ELIZABETH MOYER

Energetic, happy, shy, helpful
Sister of William
One who loves dogs, rabbits, and my family
Who feels happy when it's summer vacation,
    playing outside and swimming
Who needs toys, rain and TV
Who gives walks to my dog, food to my rabbit,
    and help to my grandma.
Who fears snakes, sharks, and spiders
Who would like to go to the Bahamas, Florida,
    and London
Resident of Pennsylvania
Moyer

                                                Elizabeth Moyer
                                                      Age: 11

BOBBY

My little baby brother is so cute,
I think he'd look so gorgeous in a suit.
When I see him I give him a kiss and a hug.
I'd like to put his picture on my mug.
I'll take pictures of me and my li'l bro,
Sled riding down big hills in the snow.

Melinda Terpilowski
Age: 11

MRS. HAUCK

Mrs. Hauck is my teacher,
She teaches English for her feature.
She is very tall,
To reach her I have to call.
She is very nice,
To my day she adds some spice.

Caitlyn Reid
Age: 11

CHEYENNE PIERCE

Libby
Energetic, shy, nice, short
Sister of Sherene
One who loves my family, Chi Chi, and music
Who feels comfortable with friends, safe with family,
   and happy with my cat
Who needs music, love, and happiness
Who gives love, care to my cat, respect to my family,
   and help to others
Who fears spiders, lighting, and jellyfish
Who would like to see the world, fly, and be invisible
Resident of Pennsylvania
Pierce

Cheyenne Pierce
Age: 13

THANKSGIVING

Thanksgiving Day is near,
And it is almost here.
I heard turkeys gobbling,
While I was wobbling.
My family went to eat Thanksgiving dinner,
And I was the winner!

> Brett Chieze
> Age: 11

The bright stars of night
Place yourself in the sky.
So when we wake up in the morning
You can keep our dreams safe.

> Julia Duncan
> Age: 11

HANNAH BUDZOWSKI

Hannah
Athletic, tall, organized, loving
Sister of Pete and Elsa Lynn
One who loves my family, my pets, and gymnastics.
Who feels happy to spend time with my friends,
   emotional on the last day of school,
   and thrilled to get good grades.
Who needs three meals a day, sleep every night,
   and a vacation every year.
Who gives food to my cats, care to my family and friends,
   and money and books to children in need.
Who fears spiders, sharks, and family members traveling
   to the other side of the world.
Who would like to travel to Japan,
   make it to the State Championships in gymnastics,
   and visit my friends in New Jersey.
Resident of Pennsylvania.
Budzowski

Hannah Budzowski
Age: 12

The crickets sing me to sleep.
The sun wakes me up to another new day.
The sky is nice and blue.
The crickets then sing me to sleep again.

Greg Lynn
Age: 11

FAITH PEARSON

Short, smart, organized, friendly.
Sister of David and Billy.
One who loves my cat and dog, my family and pizza.
Who needs food, water, shelter, and air.
Who gives food to my cat and dog, love to my family
   and to my friends.
Who fears spiders, tornadoes, and loud alarms.
Who would like to visit my cousin in Colorado,
   go to New York (again), and go to a water park
Resident of Pennsylvania.
Faith Pearson

Faith Pearson
Age: 11

EMILY RIGOTTI

Emily,
Cheerful, caring, helpful, exciting
Sister of Sam and Luke
One who loves my family, soccer and writing poems.
Who feels happy to help others, nervous to start school,
   mad when my brother hits me.
Who needs soccer, food, and television
Who gives toys to my little brother, food to my cats,
   and hugs to my mom and dad
Who fears sharks, spiders and big millipedes.
Who would like to become an author,
   write beautiful poems and sell my books.
Resident of Pennsylvania
Rigotti

                                            Emily Rigotti
                                              Age: 11

GIGGLE QUEEN

A giggle here
A chuckle or two there
When you laugh I'm with you
When you laugh I'm laughing, too.
I am the giggle queen
not to be mean
When you say you're always sad
you lie and make me a little mad
I heard you before
I hear you laugh at least once more
No one can be sad all the time
No one can always rhyme
But I will not scream or shout
Giggle queen over and out

Autumn James

FIRES AND WIND

The fire dances as the wind sings to it,
The fire gets tired and dies down,
But the wind sings louder and louder.

Austin Goehring
Age: 11

Ladybugs, ladybugs
Are talking to me.
Butterflies, butterflies
Are walking to me.
Caterpillars, caterpillars
Are squigglin' to me.

Can you tell it's spring?

Lindsay Rae McCowin
Age: 12

THE OCEAN

The ocean waves kissed my feet.
Washing away my problems, cares, and worries
for the moment.
The beach is a beautiful treasure
with its glimmering gold sand.
The ocean is so pure, so true
and a lovely shade of blue.
The lovely orange sunset shining over the water
reflecting onto your face.
After you leave you realize why you came.

Olivia Robinson
Age: 11

WINTER'S RAIN

Snow comes down like feathers,
floating through the sky.
It's the greatest of all weathers,
starting from way up high.

The sun melts it away,
before we get to laugh and play.
The snow keeps my hopes up
that it might come another day.

Cristina Maria Perrotta
Age: 11

The leaves of fall
are on a ball
falling off trees
like fleas chasing bees.

They were changing colors
faster than a cheetah's mother.
The beautiful colors of fall
will soon be turning to snow
before we know it.

The leaves of fall

                                            Sinead McAnallen
                                                       Age: 12

AMERICAN VETERANS

A re heroes
M any lives taken away
E xtraordinary fighters
R espect the U.S.
I ndependence
C ry for freedom
A lways remembered
N ever forgotten
S erve the United States of America

                                                 Briana Ferrucci
                                                      Age: 12

I get on the block
and stare down my opponents
and as the buzzer sounds
I dive in and start to stroke
and as I begin to pull away
I feel like a million dollars.
As I come to the wall
I do my flip turn
and come to find
that I'm way ahead
and I win the race.

    Swim meets

Eric McCall
Age: 12

IF I COULD BE AN ANIMAL

If I could be an animal it would be
Something that could fly like a bumble bee,
Or something that can roar really loudly
Like a big gigantic lion that's cowardly,
Or something that could spy
Like a big black, hairy, gigantic fly,
Or something that could shake
Like a big gigantic snake.
All of this thinking makes me tired
Ohh ohh I think I'm wired.

Ashley Miller
Age: 12

Rachel
Tall, polite, organized
Sister of Chuck, Alaina, and Adrianne
One who loves dancing, music, and my family
Who feels excited to meet new people,
   anxious to go to bed, and cranky in the morning
Who needs sleep, free time and new pointe shoes
Who gives love to my family,
   my best effort all the time,
   and helps my diabetic sister
Who fears spiders, clowns, and sharks
Who would like to visit the American Ballet Theatre,
   meet Green Day, and learn to play the guitar and bass
Resident of Pennsylvania
Sapienza

Rachel Sapienza
Age: 12

There was a little mouse,
with a pretty pink blouse.
Wherever it blew,
the mouse always knew,
the blouse didn't blow in the house.

>Karley Anne Houston
>Age: 10

Shark
mean fish
feeding, biting, swimming
It can attack and kill people.
Man-eater

>Curtis Wysocki
>Age: 10

As thou ride away on a gallant horse
Tears fill up my eyes
When thou are gone, my heart skips a beat.
Why has he gone?
When will he come back to me?

I sleep with dread and grief.
No news on Sir Lancelot.
I dream of him.
His voice is a mysterious sound in my head.
I fear the worst has yet to come to thee.

I am now back in his strong arms.
Safe and comfort has filled thee.
He hands me his spear,
Which is still warm from thy grasp.
He looks up to thy yonder sky.
He is home.

Elicia Gibson
Age: 12

There once was a cow.
He always said now.
The cow said moo.
So how do you do?
And then ran away with the sow.

Marissa M. Mihalcin
Age: 9

Cow
black, white
eating, mooing, lying
They were moving in the field
Calf

Brittney Rogan
Age: 10

Fire, talk and I will listen.
Water, guide me to the sea.
Sky, remind me to breathe.
Sun, bring me light to make me see.
Moon, dream me to sleep.
Stars, show your light
and I will see you glitter in the night.

Logan McDonald
Age: 12

My mom is so nice.
I hope she doesn't have lice.
I love my mommy.

Delaney D. David
Age: 9

FOOTBALL

I wish I went to a game,
That was played in Notre Dame.
When I watched there was a fight,
About the football brown and white.
There was a pass that was incomplete,
It was overturned and then complete.

Andrew Uram
Age: 11

SAVIOR

S aved our country
A lways there
V eterans
I n service
O h, how honorary
R espectful

Nick Holmes
Age: 11

BOY AND GIRL

A boy likes rough football.
A girl likes to cheer for boys.
A boy likes tough baseball and basketball.
A girl likes cool softball.
A boy carries a wallet.
A girl carries a pretty purse.
A boy likes kickball.
A girl likes soccer.
A boy likes loud dirt bikes.
A girl likes shoe shopping.

Alyson Page Pierce
Age: 9

BASEBALL

Baseball is fun.
Baseball is cool.
Do you like to run?
You get out of school.

Do you like to hit?
Try not to fall.
Do your shoes fit?
Let's play ball!

Joseph Palladino
Age: 10

There once was a cat named Chuck.
Who heard a turkey cluck.
He amazed them all.
When he made the turkey fall.
Into all the muddy muck.

                                                      Dylan DeSilvey
                                                          Age: 9

MY CAT

My cat is like a fluff ball.
She is as quiet as a tiny puppy.
She makes me happy when she tries to catch a leaf.
My cat is as brown as a tree trunk
with stripes as black as night.
She makes me feel happy.
I love my cat!

                                            David John Johnson
                                                          Age: 9

(HAPPY HOLIDAYS)

I love fall so much, so much
I love it more than buttercups
I see you near
I want to scream
I know it's almost Halloween

Winter is near these days I know
Because they're filled with so much snow
I need it gone for every day
Except for every holiday

Halloween with all its ghouls
Thanksgiving comes, we're out of school
Christmas comes with all its cheer
Then will come a brand-new year

So now with the holidays so very near
It sometimes brings a happy tear
Families together from distant coasts
Let's raise our glass in a happy holiday toast

(Happy Holidays)

Megan Jamison
Age: 11

My dad is so fun.
I like my dad very much.
I'm glad he's my dad.

Aerial Pratt
Age: 9

Clarinets, like slick black dresses
Where it flares at the bottom,
With silver buttons all over.
They enjoy singing beautiful high-pitched notes,
And like being accompanied by the piano.

Lisa Giancola
Age: 12

Star, glitter upon the night sky,
Dance around the Milky Way.
Gaze into my bedroom window,
And show me your bright light.

Roxanne Beall
Age: 12

PANDA BEAR

A panda bear with very long hair,
Was flying in the air.
I looked back so I wouldn't get slapped
By a big panda bear.
When he landed he gave me a hug
And when he stopped and I looked up.
He flew away.

Joscelyn Park
Age: 10

I HAVE

I have climbed the tallest mountains,
I have drunk from many fountains.
I have fought for many lords,
I have fought with many swords.
I have conquered all the lands,
I have traveled all the sands.

Tyler Matteo
Age: 12

The moon sits in the sky,
While it waits for the sun to come.
The spoon stays in the drawer,
While it waits to be used.
The newspaper lays in the paper company,
While it waits to be read.
The snow twinkles in the sky,
While it waits to be played in.

Alexander Grymes
Age: 12

There once was a guy named Wayne.
He traveled and came from Spain.
He rode a bike.
Then he took a hike.
Then he hurried and caught a train.

                                            Eric Mastrianno
                                                        Age: 10

DOMINICK CALDARARO

Dom
Athletic, small fast cool.
Brother of David and Joe
Who loves junk food dirt bikes sports and his family.
Who feels happy about sports
   sad about wars scared about spiders.
Who need food in his stomach his dirt bike and family.
Who gives money to the poor candy to his brothers
   love to his family.
Who would like to meet Travis Pastrana
   tame a raccoon meet the New England Patriots
Resident of Pennsylvania
Caldararo

                                      Dominick Caldararo
                                                  Age: 12

I love the ocean
The waves come in beautifully
The crests are the best.

Shelby Zager
Age: 9

MY JEWELRY BOX

The diamonds on my earrings
are as bright as shining stars.
The pearls on my necklace
are like a creamy bowl of pudding.
The beads on my bracelet are as hard as a rock.
My jewelry box is as soft as a tiger's skin.
When my jewelry box is dropped,
it sounds like a thunderstorm.
My gold chain is like the sun shining down on the earth.
The corners on my jewelry box
are as sharp as a pointed table.
My jewelry box has pink gems
like my pink walls in my bedroom.
My jewelry box is as beautiful as pink roses.

Hannah Rochelle Diaz
Age: 8

MY DOG BEAU

My dog is mostly as white as a cloud.
When he goes outside he smells
as if he was just in the mud.
He looks like a cotton ball when he's clean.
He feels like a fluffy blanket.
He makes me feel like a dog too.

Marissa Miller
Age: 8

Cats
soft, fur
hissing, meow, purring
The kitten is brown
Feline

Olivia Beveridge
Age: 10

INSIDE--OUTSIDE

Inside you can watch TV.
Outside you can see Mother Nature.

Inside there is a kitchen.
Outside there is a playground.

Inside you can be in a room.
Outside you can be in the air.

Inside there is a plug.
Outside there is not.

Inside you can twirl a baton.
Outside you can Hula-Hoop.

Inside you can sit on a bed.
Outside you can sit on the ground.

Ashley Blanchard
Age: 9

SAD--HAPPY

I am sad when you are mean.
I am happy when you are caring.

I am sad when someone dies.
I am happy when they are with me.

I am sad when nobody plays.
I am happy when everybody plays.

I am sad when my mom is not home.
I am happy when my mom is home.

Makenna Snyder
Age: 8

DARK--LIGHT

In the dark you can't see,
In the light you can see.
In the dark it's not bright,
In the light it is bright.
In the dark you walk,
In the light you can run.
In the dark you are careful,
In the light you are carefree.

Kevin Kite
Age: 8

There once was a boy who was nine
Who had cross-country on his mind
He races home to get on his running shoes
He refuses to lose
He will race you to the finish line

Chris Mastrianno
Age: 9

Dogs
noisy, loud
happy, running, playing
They play all day long.
Mammals

Kaitlyn Beck
Age: 10

MY FISH HUNTER

It is as gray as the clouds on a rainy day.
His body is as cold as a glass of milk.
It is as soft as a mouse.
It smells like a river.
It feels scaly like a snake.
When I feel it I get tingly like touching a chalkboard.

>William R. Daniels
>Age: 8

There once was a girl named Molly,
Who liked to feel jolly,
She would laugh all day,
Until the sun set away.
Then she went home to her collie.

>Molly Stonebraker
>Age: 9

My family
always happy
smiling, singing, dancing
Always ready for something new.
Picture perfect

Jessica Klumph
Age: 9

Mom
always kind
singing, working, baking
My mom is very, very nice
Nancy

Amelia Hemminger
Age: 9

Pittsburgh Steelers,
making the highlight reelers.
They have the power
under the rule of Bill Cower.

Adam Hubert
Age: 9

Uncle Nate I love you
For all the things you do.
Even though you pick on me
I love you can you see!!

Lisa Wilson
Age: 9

MY MOM'S FISH

My mom's fish is as ugly as a hairball.
It has a white face.
It has bulging eyes like a frog.
It has a brown circle on his back like an eye.
It has a red stomach like red ink.
It has blue fins like the sea.
I think my mom needs to clean the bowl.

Brody A. McFall
Age: 8

I saw trees last night
They were tall, but best of all
I found my lost kite.

Michael Comninos
Age: 9

There once was a man
that had a can filled with sand.
He walked to the sea
and bumped his knee.
He cleaned it up with his hand.

Hunter Coombs
Age: 10

MY DOG BULLET

His fur color is like a dark room.
He sounds like a thunderstorm.
He smells like he took a bath in the sewer.
He looks like a hairy monster.
He feels like a soft cloud in the sky.
He makes me feel happy.

David Struble
Age: 9

YELLOW

Yellow is the sun in the sky
that makes me want to sleep on my pillow.
It's also the shining of a tree of willow.
It's the color of the Steelers' sign
on the helmets upon their heads
like the color of my bed.
Butter is also yellow and makes food creamy.
Butter really makes batter dreamy.
Yellow is my favorite color of all!

Russell James Titus
Age: 10

MY CAT

My cat is like the color of white snow.
She looks like fluffy clouds.
She makes me feel happy.
She smells like cotton candy.
My cat's nose is cold as snow.
She sounds like a motor when she purrs.
She likes to taste her new food.
My cat eats like a pig.

Alexandra Sanders
Age: 8

RED

Ruby red is my birthstone color
it's also the color of the flowers of my mother.
A dark red rose is the big sister of pretty pink.
Red is a beautiful color don't you think?
When you look at the American flag
do the bright red stripes stand out to you?
When I look at my feet I see my cute red shoes!
When my little baby cousins take a nappy
they normally sleep with a red blanky!
At Redbank football games
the white and red colors are the best.
When it comes to red this color could win any test.
That is why red is the best!!!

Morgan Toth
Age: 9

HORSES

Going, going to the top,
Running, running fast as lightning,
Going so fast I think I'm flying,
Flying, flying, flying higher,
Flying so fast the ground is on fire,
Your horse's love will stay forever.

Jessica Gander
Age: 11

BLUE

Blue is the color of the sky
and the way I feel when I'm up high.
It is the brightest color in the crayon box.
It is also the color of your socks.
My eyes are blue and yours might be too.
Blue is the color of some balloons.
I hope to see the color blue soon.
It's the color of your jeans
and the color of some jellybeans.
I think of blue when I get cold.
It's like the house that just got sold.
My favorite color is truly blue!

Kevin Eberle Jr.
Age: 10

THE FALL

I like the different colors of the leaves
Red, orange, brown and green.
I like the different colors
Because they are so pretty.
I like to jump in the leaves every fall.
Every fall I like to rake them up.
I like fall because it is so fun!!!

William Dalton Piacitelli
Age: 6

CONE OF SILENCE

I see their lips moving
But no one speaks
I am in a world silence
So isolated and confused
Won't somebody help me
Set my life straight
I want to be normal
Lead a good life
To at least know what it's like
But I can't
For I am different
From everyone else
I live in a cone of silence
So confused
I am screaming out loud
But nobody hears
I don't know why
But it is true
I live in a cone of silence
All confused

Becca Sue Delair

PETS

My sister's dog is Ben
and when we got him he was sent in a pen
My dog is Ash he doesn't like his sash
My cat is Hobbes
he's mischievous
and I named him after "Calvin & Hobbes"
My sister's cat is Bo and he attacked my father's toe
My sister's hamster is named Ashley
and she almost bit my cat's knee
My hamster's name is Hammy
and she likes to be held by my mother Tammy
We only have one fish
because the other was my cat's main dish
These are my pets and they don't like to go to the vets

Skyler McHenry
Age: 12

MY DIRT BIKE

It has two wheels like a super bike.
It sounds like a car when it is running.
It is red like my blanket.
It is as hot as a fire when you ride it a lot.
It is as cold as a freezer when you haven't ridden it yet.
It makes me feel like I never felt before.

Nathan Patten
Age: 8

GREEN

A green crayon is the color of spring
and the color of a dragon's wing.
Green is the color of sticky hair gel
and the look of a weathered cow's bell.
Green is the color of a school folder
and the look of a penny that's older.
Green is the color of a shirt that I wear.
Have you ever seen anyone with green hair?
Green is the color of a car it's the best color by far!!!

Gabe Troup
Age: 9

VIEW FROM HEAVEN

It's nighttime and I'm trying to sleep
But when I think about you I cry and weep
Suddenly I think about the brighter days
The happiness and laughter . . . my memories with you
will NEVER fade away
Because I'm thinking of you, I try to smile
And it's hard to remember because I haven't seen you
in a long while
Two long years have gone past and I wonder . . .
Will my sadness always last?
But I'm looking up to you up there in a brighter place
I finally see your face
Smiling because you're looking down on me from Heaven

In memory of Ryan

Haley Eisenman
Age: 12

ART

Art is creative
Art is a masterpiece
Art is fun
Art is a hobby of mine
But art is more
Art is more than creativity
Art is more than having fun
Art is more than a hobby
Art is my life
You take art away
And you're taking
My life away,
My dignity
And my pride.

Dedicated to Mr. Shaffer to show him how much
I appreciate all the hard work he does. Thanks a lot,
you made my life mean something and someday
I hope to be an artist and it's all because of Mr. Shaffer.

Ashley Marie Little

RED

Red is a color of a valentine heart,
and it's the color of my favorite Pop Tart.
Red is the glowing color of mice eyes
and my dad's suit tie.
Red is an apple so juicy and bright
that's in a tree because it is ripe.
Red is a color of a rose that grows from the ground,
and a stop sign that stands on the way to town.
Red is like my bed, so comfy and soft,
and the color of my chair that I sit on,
at my school or in my loft.
I am full of glee, as you can see;
red is the color for me.

Rita Ann Nolf
Age: 10

PINK

Pink is a favorite color of girls.
It is also the color of beautiful pearls.
When I look at pink it makes me happy.
It's the color of my baby cousin's blankey.
I love to chew pink bubblegum.
If I had a choice I would give it two thumbs!
It is the color of shiny lipstick.
I put it on as the clock goes tick, tick, tick.
The pink crayon sticks out in the box
just like pink forget-me-nots.
I like flowers that are pink.
Pink is the best color don't you think?

Ashley Mangiantini
Age: 9

BEAVERS

Beavers are cool
they like to swim in my pool
their teeth like to gnaw
just like a saw,
their tails are flat
so they can use 'em as a bat
their fur is brown
that's why they don't like to frown
   Beavers are cool

Molly Beth Wise
Age: 12

GOLD

A king's crown is gold
and so is an old paper fold.
Gold is the color of a kind person's soul.
It's also the same color of my dad's tools.
Gold is the color of my mom's sparkling rings
and the colors of the gifts Santa brings.
The crisp golden sun
shines on me when I run.
Gold makes me free.
It's the color for me!

Kara Hatch
Age: 10

PIE

The crust is as light brown as dust.
It is as hot as the sun, when it comes out of the oven.
Sometimes if you put it in a cooler
It gets as cold as an ice cube.
It tastes as good as ice cream.
It smells as good as a flower.
It looks as good as cake.
It makes me feel good.

Heather Zacherl
Age: 9

FEAR AT THE DOOR

A young Jewish girl am I,
From the Nazis I must hide,
Horror is racing through my mind,
I am too young to die.
My family must hide down here,
In a dark basement full of fear,
Everyone is shedding silent tears,
As we hear them coming near.
Our friends that keep us in hiding,
Must tell them there's no one down here, but they're lying,
To keep us safe they're trying,
But suddenly I hear a woman crying.
Then suddenly the door swings open,
No words from my mouth are spoken,
I pray that there is a token,
To get out of this place that keeps me choking.
And from the sound of a gun roar,
The man falls to the floor,
We race out of the door,
In search of a place to hide once more.

Rebekah Jayne Keister
Age: 13

FOOTBALL

The quarterback calls the play then walks up to the line,
But then he notices that he said the wrong sign.
So he calls a time-out and says "here's how we win,"
The coach stood on the sideline with a big grin.
The center snaps the ball and takes a step back,
He trips the quarterback and knocks him down for a sack.
The center got called out after the play,
His coach told him to stay out of the quarterback's way.
So he drops back for a pass,
And throws it to his wide receiver 'cause he is so fast.
The receiver caught the ball and ran with a grin,
He danced into the end zone for a big win!

Garrett McCleary
Age: 13

GREEN

Christmas trees are the color of green
and so is the color of other trees.
Green is the color of peas in a pod.
Green is the color of a house made of sod.
It is the color of money in a bank
and the color of a U.S. Army Tank.
Green is the color of a garden snake.
Green can be the color of icing on a cake.
Green is my favorite color of all!

Lynde D. Edmonds
Age: 9

CHEERLEADING

Cheerleaders are awesome
They can throw 'em and toss 'em
We feel the heat but stay with the beat
We cheer and we greet our uniforms are neat
We jump and we stunt
We say things like touchdown score six more
We rock and knock you down
We are the best
Cheerleading

Brandi Colwell
Age: 13

YESTERDAY

Yesterday I hit my head
When I fell out of my bed
I got orange juice in my eye
And also I dropped a pie
I cracked the TV in half
And then I tripped the baby calf
The pigs all chased me when I stole some mud
And I hit the ground with a big thud
I also got stung by a bee
Yesterday was hard as you can see

Tyler Powell
Age: 11

MISSING WORLD

The sun's enraged
The moon's in grief
The stars are worried
All order is gone
And with it is the Earth
Please come back Earth
We need and miss you
Please
O ... KAY ...

Matthew Haines
Age: 11

MUSIC

There's something all around us,
It's ringing through the air,
When it is surrounding me,
I've not got a single care.

From a concert to a jukebox,
Music is so soothing.
It stimulates my inner thoughts,
To me it is very moving.

So many different rhythms,
Notes of all different kinds.
Once I hear a great song,
I can't get it out of my mind.

Some tempos fast and upbeat
Others very slow,
With notes of so many tones,
Some high pitched, and some down low.

Music is all around us,
This I know is true.
Take the time to stop and think,
How does music affect you?

Michael Miller
Age: 12

DAYDREAM

I get lost in my head
fixed in a daydream
sometimes
they are the best
sometimes
they are nightmares
but either way
I am reminded of what I miss
You

Thria Jordan Devlin
Age: 12

DRAWING

I love to draw, I love art,
just a few lines is the way to start
You can draw anything you'd like
it could be a tree, or even a bike
Anything you want to draw is fine,
you do not have to copy mine
So do not rush or even hurry,
you know you'll just get in a flurry
Now just relax and have some fun,
and show me when your drawing is done

Esther O'Connor
Age: 11

A WEDDING NIGHT

At the door
before my eyes
for me to see
until I die
upon the stars
around the planets
under my bed
during the night
for it was
throughout my mind
beyond my reach
inside my head
since I was wed

Christin Foster
Age: 12

BLUE

Blue is the color of my dirt bike
and the sky when you take a hike.
You can hear the ocean when the blue waves crash
and you may see a bright blue flash.
Blueberries fall off the tree.
Blue is the color of my birthstone
and some people's telephones.
Blue is the brightest color in the box.
It's also the color of Paul Bunyan's ox.
Blue is a great color for me!

Kaven Isaac Hornberger
Age: 9

I SEE THE RAINBOW

I see the rainbow's colors every day
I see RED, the color of my Christmas sleigh
I can see ORANGE the color of the clay
The sun is a nice bright YELLOW
My brother eats bright GREEN Jell-O
I wear jeans that are a dark BLUE
I wear a light PURPLE shirt, too
I see RED, ORANGE, YELLOW, GREEN, BLUE,
and PURPLE

Rebecca Cochran
Age: 12

Let's go on a Thanksgiving adventure
Are you ready? Are you sure?
Where will we adventure to?
How about the deep and murky blue?

Or what about the sky?
We can't go there we can't fly
Then how about the pool?
I wish we could go there but it is too cool.

Then what about the woods?
Yea to catch some turkey goods,
Grab your cork gun,
Come on let's run!

"We're going to get hungry,
Too bad Mom is not done with the turkey
So grab some chips,
Aw, man no French onion dip."

We'll need some bait
"We better leave a note, what is the date?"
Mom yells "careful"
After we have a belly full

Let's head to the forest
This is so fun that even the boredest
Kid would have a good time
After this we could sell turkey meat by the dimes

There is a turkey
We'll make it into jerky
Stuff it full
And eat it until,

We burst with fun
Shoot that gun
Now bring him home
And watch out for that garden gnome

Put him in a pot
Place him in the oven to keep him hot
Cook him good, later we'll eat
Time to watch football see who they'll beat

How about doing some crafts
Yes mine will get tons of laughs
With the kitchen smells
Who would guess turkey, well that's swell?

With the blessing said for our food
What a great and happy mood
For this great delicious turkey
That was hunted to make jerky

And the greatest meal around
And has this great party sound
So thanks to all the givers
Like this turkey that slept by rivers

> Sydney Crago
> Age: 11

FALL

I love fall.

With all the leaves crunching under my feet
and leaves blowing all over the street.

With leaves changing color.

The smell of pumpkin pie
makes me feel like I'll never die.

When winter's near the leaves will die
                            Y.
                         L
and the wind will may them F

                                      Nicholas Thornton
                                      Age: 10

MY DOG

My dog smells so clean--just like me.
He was born to be wild.
He can run as fast as a roadrunner.
He can jump over a fence like a kangaroo.
He is as strong as a great white shark.
He can swim as fast as a swimmer.
He can sing to the moon just like wolves do at night.

                                        Anna Rose Zrile
                                        Age: 9

FALL

In the fall, leaves are falling,
   there are also turkeys calling.
To the south the birds are flying,
   as all of the bushes are dying.
Footballs are being thrown and punted,
   as all of the animals are being hunted.
All of the kids have gone trick-or-treating,
   for a load of candy, they could be eating.
My favorite sport, hockey, is just beginning,
   and my favorite team is always winning.
These are some of the reasons,
   why fall is my favorite season.

Trevor Rodgers
Age: 9

REESE

Extremely small
Very lovable
Superly playful
Beautiful fur
Sharp claws
Licks treats
Super sweet
Sometimes independent

Kalysta Greer
Age: 11

POEMS

Poems big poems small,
Ones that don't rhyme at all.
Poems happy poems sad,
Poems that make me really mad!

Poems easy poems hard,
Poems written in a card.
Haiku, shape, and cinquain!
Acrostic, alliteration, and quatrain!

Many poems different sizes.
Many poems different prizes!
Some ugly some pretty,
Some that are very witty.

Some about night some about day,
Some about sleeping in the hay!
Some about winter some about spring,
Some about pretty much anything!

Some about summer some about fall,
Some about nothing at all!
Poems big poems small,
Like them, love them, read them all!!!

Samantha Nicole Rowden
Age: 11

THE BEDROOM

In the bedroom
A lot of things
There's a table
With water
And pretty paintings
With a bed
That's comfortable
I just am thinking of
Myself sleeping
This is the best thing
I want in my
Life

Riquel Corder
Age: 8

THE WIND

The wind
You make trees sing and dance
You make waves swish back and forth
You make the clouds move to another place
You make my hair swish in my face
You make the dandelion seeds move from place to place
You make the bird's feathers blow away with you
That is the end of the wind

Martha B. Parris
Age: 9

SHE IS A WRITER

She is a writer
who gets her feelings out
by writing for the paper
about teen moms,
baby-sitting--you name it.

She is a writer
who expresses herself
through her works of art
that she keeps to herself
most of the time.

She is a writer
whose accomplishments
sing from the depths of her heart
and receive many compliments
when she lets others hear her song.

She is a writer
who inspires herself daily
and pushes herself to
work harder all the time.
That writer is me.

Alaina Rydzewski
Age: 15

FISHING ALONE

The fish is gold
The water is sparkling
Fishing is not
As fun as you
THINK
It is really
Peaceful and quiet
As it can be
Fishing alone is
Very peaceful
You can hear
Birds chirping
Wind blowing
Fishing alone is
Very fun you see!

Patrick Tebalt
Age: 8

FISHING IN THE SPRING

Spring is here
Birds are coming it's time to fish
The water is cool all the fish are out
You can see everything
The bridge is so high
The sun is nice and sweet
It is so cold outside
It is so beautiful out
You can see the trees dancing
Because of the wind blowing
Fishing in the spring

Jade Burroughs
Age: 8

IN THE FALL

Fall you can see the leaves falling from the trees.
You can hear the crunch from the leaves under your feet.
Fall you can jump in the leaves but when you do
you can hear the leaves sounding like bushes in the wind.
You get to play football
and get to be all muddy, cold, and wet.
Fall means you get to taste all of the food
from Thanksgiving.
You get to hear all of your friends.

Sebastian Rinehardt
Age: 10

THE CHAIR IS COMFY

The chair is so sweet
And comfortable, soft
You just want to
Sit down
And go to sleep
Wake up in
Two days!
You will never
Get UP out
Of the chair
Ever!

Keishawn Wentz
Age: 8

THE SOUNDS

The sounds the cars make
So peaceful
When the water sways
Back and forth
What the leaves make
People talking
It's so peaceful
Water with a person in it

Devin Stokes
Age: 9

WHERE IS TURKEY?

I'm playing hide-and-seek.
I'll try not to peek.
Where's Turkey?
For Turkey is hiding
should I name him Clyding?
He's not here. He's not there.
Turkey's not anywhere!
Mama says it's time to eat.
I stomp my feet because . . .
I can't find Turkey!!!
My brother Lurkey saw Turkey . . .
along with Beef Jerky . . .
In the oven!!!

Mackenzie Conrad
Age: 9

THE CHAIR

The chair is soft
It is warm and hot
The chair is comfortable
It is relaxing
The chair is brown and black
The chair

Sean T. Johnson Jr.
Age: 9

WINTER

Winter, winter.
Soft snow on the ground.
Christmas presents
under the beautiful tree.
New toys
that Santa and elves left there.

Christmas carolers
sing a tune.
While we clean up
wrapping paper,
I go outside
and play in the snow.
I mount up
the snow hill.
I go back inside
to eat pie.

I smell food
in the fresh air.
We eat turkey,
Christmas candy,
and hot chocolate.

Delanie Kelly
Age: 9

WINTER

The sign of white snow is wintry and bitter plus,
with it covered all around,
it looks like Vermont in Altoona but,
don't you love to see the houses decorated for the season,
it's so pretty and joyful
I also love to see hills and hills of snow
I feel so peaceful
but when I hear the wind blow
"Brrr" I'm cold
I love to hear the snow fall
it sounds like a Thump, Thump, Thump
and the bells ringing Jingle, Jingle, Jingle
with snow everywhere
it's so beautiful but when I touch it I'm ice cold,
when I touch turkey and hot cocoa I'm frying
I despise cold cocoa
I have a craving for turkey at Christmas
with roast beef, cookies and hot cocoa it's stupendous
I hate the smell of old snow
It smells like an old damp washrag
but, the fireplace smells like wood
white snow is cold the fireplace is warm,
and green is smooth
sprinting in the snow is cold
and fun helping one another
feels good and great inside
but making cookies is fun, happy, and joyful.

Sarah Balmforth
Age: 9

CHRISTMAS MORNING

One day I woke up with such a twinkle in my eye,
It was like seeing the North Star
In the sea of the dark, night sky.
"It's Christmas," I shouted as loud as I possibly could.
Then I ate a Christmas cookie and said,
"Mom these are so good!"
Then I ran downstairs
Just as fast as my little feet would go.
That's when I saw the presents stacked from head to toe.
I opened up the first one and to my own surprise;
It was a very pretty doll with big blue eyes.
"It's gorgeous," I said with a big huge smile.
"I've wanted this for quite some while."
"I know," said my mom with a mile-long grin,
"That's the way Santa's been time and time again."
Now as I sit upon my couch with my little doll,
I know that Santa's not a fake, not a fake at all,
And even as the years go on and I am growing old,
I know my faith in Santa Claus will always be bold.

Ashley Reynolds
Age: 11

WINTER WONDERLAND

The snow feels cold between my fingers
hills of snow lay peacefully before me
glistening in the late afternoon sunlight.
Snow creeping down a hill
makes me shiver with excitement.
When Christmas carolers come to my doorstep and sing
I think of singing with them sometimes
as the hot chocolate trickles down my throat
it makes me feel warm inside.
I get excited when new toys arrive
as bells ring on top of sleighs
the sound brings me joy
when it gets too cold outside
my winter coat keeps me warm
the delicious cookies
my mother makes
taste like a dream
the ham my mom cooks
is very scrumptious
as the cookies bake
the wonderful smell spreads
the white wonderland
in my dream
will be real someday.

Haleigh Schmidhamer

THE LITTLE WHITE BOAT

I listen to the waves.
The calm, soothing, sound
is comforting and relaxing;
it's quiet all around.

I feel the sand between my toes.
I bury them into the ground.
I feel something different
and look to see what I found.

I pick something up
out of the sand
and hold it very tight
in the palm of my hand.

It's a little white boat
that someone sent out to sea
putting all their worries on it
which strangely came to me.

So remember you're not the only one
that has troubles and cares
and take some time out of your life
and just say a little prayer.

Alyssa Beck
Age: 13

Winter
how beautiful you are
your bright white snow
and your clear blue sky
sleds go darting
in your white delight
your hills of snow
glitter in your light
kids laugh and dash
and have fun
snowballs fly
your snow is freezing
snowballs are tempting
your ice is frozen
when it is close
to your holiday
people bake cookies
and drink milk
when your coldness
is at your most
people make
HOT CHOCOLATE
Winter
your red and green colors
recall your holiday
Christmas
white reminds me
of snow
all of your colors
fill me of good
Christmas decorations

Christian Snyder
Age: 9

OUR BAND

I have a pet llama and we started a band.
We play everywhere like the jungle and on the sand.
The band's gonna last forever like the Rolling Stones.
At every concert we give out free ice cones.
The day we break up it's gonna be sad.
We're gonna remember all the good times we had.
One more thing, I forgot to tell you the name,
We're the Llama Lords, the name's cool not lame.

Zachary T. Kraus
Age: 11

FOOTBALL

I can feel the wind in my face
when I run up and down
trying to make a touchdown.

I run and push through the other team
with all my might.
I really put up a tremendous fight.

When I run out of breath,
I fall on my knees
and wait for a cool breeze.

Brett Schmitt
Age: 12

QUAD

There once was a quad that was very fast,
Went in a race and came in last,
The guy got mad and went home,
And a lot of aggression was shown,
He went to his garage and looked at his quad,
He kept looking at it and then he felt very odd,
Then he closed his eyes in shame,
And looked up and saw a new quad in the lane!

Michael Jeremy Ryan
Age: 11

MR. FORGET

There once was a guy
Who was wearing a pink tie.
He went to a dance
And forgot his pants.
All the people laughed
So he went home to take a bath!

David Yough
Age: 11

FREEDOM

Birds fly south for the winter,
and I wished that I could too.
I feel like my world is spinning around,
and I never know what to do.

When I go home I go to my room
where my blanket lay.
I hug it tight and think very hard
about my puzzling day.

Birds are so free
and can fly anywhere.
While I'm not free to spread my wings
and learn to fly without a care.

I know that I could flourish if
I could only try.
Life would be different,
if I could only fly.

Rebecca Potopa
Age: 7

HOCKEY

Hockey is the game that I love to play.
I'm at the ice rink every day.
When I lace up my skates and step on the ice,
The wind blowing by feels so nice.

It feels good when I skate really fast,
But as soon as I'm there, the puck flies past.
I think to myself, "I'll get another try."
When it comes, I won't let it go by.

It feels good when I finally score
Especially when I hear the crowd roar.
We win as a team, and we lose as a team,
But whatever happens we'll always gleam.

Josh Porta
Age: 7

NIGHTMARES

Worms here, worms there, worms everywhere
Under the rugs, horrible bugs.
In the mugs, under the table!
This is no fable.
How do I get them out?
So many worms I can't shout!
I can't move at all.
The only place is in the hall.
Inch by inch I move along.
The door is shut.
Is there something wrong?
The door is locked!
I can't get through!
Help! Help! I can't breathe!
It is true
They are choking me!
I can't even see!
Then I hear the door open.
I open my eyes the worms are gone!
I figure out it was just a dream.
Back to bed with me!

Emmett Eldred
Age: 10

MY BAD DOG

My dog Hershey bites and fights.
He yips and yaps in his crate at night.
He chews, bad news.
He takes a snooze.
It seems like he can't get anything right!
He destroys my toys and eats my food.
He makes a lot of noise, noise, noise!
What's that?
He's sitting?
He's lying down?
This time when I look at him, I don't frown.
He's sitting quietly, and he gives me his paw.
Maybe this dog is not so bad after all!

Alexa Overdorff
Age: 11

A FRIEND NOT FORGOTTEN

He was a friend who understood my pain.
Without him life's just not the same.
His spirit was tame,
Now who's to blame?
'Cause cancer took its toll,
On his kind loving soul.

Brian Helsley
Age: 11

EMPTINESS

Sorrow all around--
So quiet, not one joyful sound.
From glee to despair--
This feeling, it doesn't compare . . .
Sadness, sorrow lost in time
All these thoughts, melting in mind.
Dreams, hopes, goals to make--
All is lost, like a big mistake.
Days to weeks to months to years,
With each of them come more and more tears
A miserable oblivion . . .
Such a cold, dark melancholy place,
Can I endure this lonely space?
Why does it have to end like this?
It is the feeling of emptiness.

Alyssa Ciccarelli
Age: 16

THE CHAIR

I sit on a chair
It's comfortable
I sit on a chair
It feels like
I'm floating on air
It is soft and nice
My chair

Kyle Ahlschlager
Age: 8

MR. TEST

There was a test
I did my best
When I had a chance
I took a glance
It was an A
I was A-OK.

Chris Wharry
Age: 12

RAIN

What is rain?
Clear dense drops battering everything on the ground
Creating a dark gloomy sky with giant puffy clouds
Producing puddles splashing with joy
The never-ending Drip-Drop, Drip-Drop
Swiftly running off roofs into the drains
Hitting windows, making leaves come off of trees
A soggy, damp, strong smell
Wipes away any animal scents whatsoever
Muggy air floating to the sky
Creating a gloomy world
Everyone in a miserable mood
Then a beautiful rainbow comes out
                That is Rain!

Jillian Damus
Age: 10

C hrist has been born
H olidays are fun like this one
R ings are given to Mom from Dad
I cicles are hanging from the roof
S ledding in the snow
T alking of praying for Christ
M aking presents for everyone
A cting good all year
S anta Claus is coming tonight

Douglas Birchard
Age: 9

THE FARM GIRL

Alas behold the sun rises
Shining down from the sky
Peeking through the treetops so high
Awaking habitats
To start a new day

As she arises from her sleep
And peers between the blind
Pleasantness of spring comes to mind
Bringing the picture of
The warm month of May

Her ears hear the chirping of birds
Singing the rhythmic noise
As perched upon a branch with poise
Sharing the goodness of
The rightful new way

And planting time begins as the
Clock strikes the seventh hour
Each seed planted becomes a flower
Or crops to be eaten
Or huge bales of hay

In the woods she becomes alone
To think and to ponder
About nature but never wonder
About what becomes of
Words nature has to say

She recalls that everybody
Has interpretations
No matter where in the nation
Of nature from on land
To under the bay

The dinner bell is sounded as
Day ends with the sunset
Behind the mountains that will get
The same attention from
Start of a new day

Emily L. Knott
Age: 15

POLAR BEARS

Big and burly polar bears
Swift and strong hunters
Lumbering along on the slippery ice.
Pads on their feet won't let them slip
And take an icy dip.
Hunting seals and penguins
On the icy circle Arctic Circle.
Hiding, blending in this bland white world,
Keeping camouflaged from hunters.
(Animals and humans alike)
Lumbering, stalking, hunting, hiding
In this bland white world.

Marie Gorman
Age: 10

WHAT IS SCHOOL?

Pencils tapping nervously while taking a test
Kindergartners jumping up and down,
   excited for their first day of class
Teachers inspiring with enthusiastic talking
Checking out books in the library, anxious to read
Painting a picture as beautiful as a flower
People playing dodge ball, throwing balls,
   looking rapidly, trying not to get hit
Fifth graders singing with Mrs. Corl, preparing for a play

Morgan Kaluza
Age: 11

FRIENDS

Friends are helpful in a way.
You have to be careful what you say.
They are the best things I've ever had.
But sometimes they can make me mad.
Some of my friends get in fights.
They always make up and say "We're tight."
They can sometimes embarrass me.
I can always say that's a slap on the knee.
It doesn't matter where we are.
I can always call my best friend a star.

Morgan Griffith
Age: 11

WHAT IS CHRISTMAS EVE?

On windowpanes the icy frost
   leaves feathered crissed and crossed
But in our house the Christmas tree
   is decorated festively
With tiny dots of colored light
   that cozy up this winter night
Christmas songs familiar slow
   play softly on the radio
Pops and hisses from the fire
   whistle with bells and the choir
My puppy is now fast asleep
   on his tummy dreaming deep
When the fire makes him hot
   he turns to warm whatever's not
Up against him on the rug
   I give my friend a gentle hug
Tomorrow's what I'm waiting for
   but I can't wait ANYMORE

M. J. Klein
Age: 10

THE STARS

When it's time for bed,
And I have said my prayers,
I wish upon the stars.
When I see the glow,
From the stars,
I feel magic,
In my hands.
I take a piece of the sun,
Then I make it a star.
When I go to bed,
I feel protected,
Because the sun is a star,
And the stars,
Brighten up my world.

Jayne Wilson
Age: 10

SOLDIERS

S aved our country.
O ur army is the best.
L oyal.
D o wonderful things.
I ndependence.
E veryone respects them.
R escuers.

Caitlyn Mendel
Age: 11

KEEP ON GOING

Keep on going when you're at your lowest.
Never give up at your slowest.

Keep on going when faith is lost,
Even if there is a cost.

Keep on going out of the dust.
Keep on trying you must, you must!

Keep on going believe in yourself.
Strive to be wise and not to be stealth.

Keep on going because life is a road.
It starts, it stops, and it changes modes.

Keep on going why stop now?
You finally made it, take a bow.

Howie Keenan
Age: 11

PIANO RECITAL

Sitting down
My fingers run across the keys
One slips!
Panicking, I try to remember what's next
I feel eyes staring at me,
Boring holes into my hands
My fingers are racing around in midair
I try not to disappoint Mom
Kerplunk!
I hit a key, making a guess
It sounds right . . .
I'm back on track.

Christie Jiang
Age: 10

LEAVES

Here come the leaves,
falling from the trees,
they do not wish to fall,
from a height so tall,
and when they hit the floor,
it's sure to be a bore,
to just sit there,
and listen to the wind roar.

Julien J. Denby
Age: 8

SKY

A vast blue ocean,
turned upside down,
and whispers to all its gazers,
"Come discover me."

Joseph G. Denby
Age: 10

FRENCH FRIES

You eat me, you love me
I'm salty and hot.
You dip me in ketchup
Do you love me or do you not?

Skylar Gordon
Age: 11

BOOKS BOOKS

Books, books, there are so many books.
Nonfiction, fiction, science fiction,
There are a lot more too.

If you don't yet read,
And you like picture books,
The library even has those too.

Ask a librarian to help you find
A book that's just right for you.

Did you know authors even get
Awards for their books?

There are so many books,
There are cookbooks,
There are even books about cooks!

Natalie Bukowski
Age: 11

MY LITTLE HOT-AIR BALLOON

Fly, fly, way up high
'til you reach the morning sky,

You're eating pie
scraping the sky with your fingers,

Listening to spirit
and even your favorite singers,

After the bright day the evening is sure to say,
"Good night, my little angel."

Megan Vonada
Age: 10

VETERANS

V ery brave
E ncouraging
T ough fighters
E veryone thanks you for your help
R eady to fight
A merica's saviors
N ever give up
S oldiers

Anthony Morrison
Age: 11

FROSTING

Frosting is on many things.
Practically on everything.
Frosting is like the ocean foam.
Lying on top of a wavy dome.
Frosting is great, frosting is good.
You should try it, you should!
Chocolate!
Vanilla!
Strawberry, too!
I love frosting.
Do you?
Any kind is good for me,
I love frosting.
Can't you see?

Jamie Salvaggio
Age: 10

TWIRLING

Fun performances
Many games
Toss turn
Catch toss
Itchy costumes
Cold metal
Rain shine

Mackenzie McGahan
Age: 11

FRIENDS FOREVER

My friends are great.
We've known each other since we were eight.

We always have lots of fun.
Sometimes we stay up until we see the morning sun.

We talk on the phone for hours and hours
as the phone bill rapidly towers.

We may get into fights,
but it's usually all right by the end of the night.

My friends are the ones that put smiles on my face.
We have memories that will never erase.

My friends mean the world to me.
Forever we will always be.

Morgan Berger
Age: 13

Basketball
cool, fun
running, dribbling, shooting
making shots
Basketball

Trevor Marcum
Age: 11

Penguins
small, cute
waddling, sliding, swimming
like a tuxedo
Bird

James Stoner
Age: 12

CHRISTMAS

I awaken on Christmas Day
I'm anxious and excited
to dash downstairs and see
what Santa had brought me
when I see those presents
under the tree
I'm tempted to open just one
but, they all weigh a ton
instead I take a piece of candy
it tastes so dandy
honey baked ham on the tabletop
looks good for me to chomp
red, white, green
covers my house
now I see
a Christmas mouse

Emilee Hollingsworth
Age: 9

AFTER SCHOOL WORK

A fter school work, is starting again.
F lattening, tiring, exhausting work that
T ests our
E xhausted brains.
R olling your eyes will not help.

S ummer is a time of no schoolwork.
C hange is coming, the school year is starting.
H omework is never done in the summer
O pen your book. September and
O ctober are times to work.
L earning is starting.

W orking during recess. Math or English
O r social studies or science and
R eading are done instead of fun.
K ickball is fun but we won't play today.

Carrie Zilhaver
Age: 9

REJOICE

The grass is green,
The air is moist,
God is the greatest,
Let's rejoice!
He created the world,
He created you and me,
Somebody who doesn't praise Him,
I wish not to see.
I see Him in my dreams,
I see Him at night,
But where I see Him most,
Is in the daylight.

Rachel M. Stetler
Age: 11

S eptember is hot.
E very day is time to play.
P lay all day.
T ries to rake the leaves.
E veryone comes over to play.
M om and Dad's party.
B ackyard baseball.
E very leaf falls off the trees.
R ains a lot.

Ciarra Peters

STARS ARE . . .

Stars are red, stars are blue
and some stars are white that look like you.
When I see the flag that flies high and proud,
it makes me feel happy all around.
Stars are red, stars are blue
and some stars are white that look like you.
Our flags stand for freedom and they can't take that away,
I am proud to be an American and that's all I can say.
Stars are red, stars are blue
and some stars are white that look like you.
When I look at the flag it reminds me
when we became free,
it's the Fourth of July that I can see.
Stars are red, stars are blue
and some stars are white that look like you.
No matter what happens our flag will always stand free.
Stars are red, stars are blue
and some stars are white that look like you.

Rebecca Johnson
Age: 11

TRINITY

Trinity
small, playful, hungry, loving
eating, playing, sniffing
my little dog
Puppy

> Max R. Toner II
> Age: 11

Logan Bechdel
fun, short
playing, talking, learning
I play baseball
Logan Bechdel

> Logan Bechdel
> Age: 11

WINTER WONDER!

Winter wonder comes alive
when people come and play outside.
When winter wonder comes next year
we will sled and play all year.
We play and play and say hey, hey, hey, yeah!
It's time to get your sled and come and play.
You don't have to pay to have fun today.
Hey, have you seen the snow today?
Play with fun and joy.
Ray is having fun today.
So come and play with Ray today.
Hey, it's time to come and play.
Hey, Fay come and play with us today.
It snows so much it does not matter,
come and play with winter wonder.
It's time to say good-bye to winter wonder.
We will see you next year in winter wonder.

Devan Sponsler
Age: 10

M any friends
A n awesome friend
C urious
Y aks a lot

                              Emily Hendricks
                                    Age: 11

                Puppies
          playful, heartbreaker
     running, playing, sleeping
           man's best friend
                Puppies

                              Taylor Jordan
                                    Age: 11

Goat
friendly, energetic
running, jumping, eating
a cool pet
Chocolate Chip

Ashley Seyler
Age: 11

WHEN I GET THERE . . .

When I am here
I see a freshly made bed.
I hear the air conditioner blowing
that sounds like a hummingbird's wings.
I feel as relaxed as if I stepped into Heaven.
I smell new bars of soap.

Ryan M. Lunsford
Age: 7

REDFORD THE DOG

Lonely, sad, feeling very bad
missing him oh dear,
that I can't talk to my peers.
Hope I can dry up all the tears
with the other dog that I love very much.
But now Redford has a family
that he loves so sweet
so he can defeat the tears in his eyes.
I really miss you Redford,
no matter what color like pink or blue even hulubaloo.
But he's red and cute.
I hope that you know this is who you are.

Michaella Francis
Age: 9

HOBBIES

Like fishing
Going exploring
Rock climbing
Riding bikes
Outside activities
Winter's great
Video games
Have fun!

Drew Tabish
Age: 11

THE CALM COUNTRY

When I am here . . .
I feel as free as a spirit.
I see waves as quiet as a mouse.
I hear a country as quiet as the seashore.
I smell sweet ocean water as nice as an air freshener.

Anthony Battaglia
Age: 7

THE TREE HOUSE

When I am here . . .
I feel as good as a dog playing catch with his owner.
I see birds flying like a parachutist in the sky.
I hear children playing like a happy bunny.
I smell fresh grass like flowers.

Claudia Harris
Age: 7

THE SUPER BOWL

What is the Super Bowl?
Coaches making plans for the next play
Scoreboard showing numbers of fear and happiness
Football players tackling, punting
   and running to the end zone
Coaches cheering for their team
Screaming people in the stands yelling for the best team
Buttery popcorn and the sweet Coke smell
Sweat of the players on the field
   and the people in the stands
The urge that you want your team to win
               That's the Super Bowl

Kayte Kocher
Age: 10

THE SWING SET

When I am here
I feel as excited as if I'm visiting a new friend.
I see the swing blowing in the breeze.
I hear the squeaking of the monkey bars.
I smell the freshly mowed green grass
that reminds me of fresh flowers.

Madison Mitchell
Age: 7

MY FAVORITE PLACE TO GO

When I am here
I feel warm water in the hot summer.
I see fawns jumping in the fields.
I hear fish splashing in the water.
I smell corn getting cut down
and it smells like sweet candy.

Dalton Barger
Age: 8

WHAT ARE FLOWERS?

Beautiful colors flowing in the breeze
Buds blooming all around
Stems of flowers bursting up from the ground
The rose stem cursing me with pain
The tiger lilies growl with rage
Gentle rustles of the flower's voice whispering in my ear
Pollen in the air the smell is everywhere
And that is a flower

Taylor Harpster

THE PEPPERMINT TREE

When I am here
I feel as happy as a monkey climbing a tree.
I see wildflowers blooming toward the sky.
I hear the chirps from a bird flying in the breeze.
I smell the peppermint leaves at Christmas Eve.

Arianna Smith
Age: 7

SCHOOL, MY SPECIAL PLACE

When I am here
I feel special when I learn really exciting new things.
I see teachers teaching in their cool breezy rooms.
I hear pencils ticking and writing
on a nice clean piece of paper.
I smell markers in the nice clean classroom.

Valerie Gulick
Age: 7

THE PLACE I LIKE TO BE

When I am here
I feel the soft warm breeze rush through me.
I see the green-bluish meadows.
I hear fresh blue water as clear as crystals
glimmering in the sunlight.
I smell fresh flowers that send their delicious aroma
into the air and the fresh smell of green pine needles.

Nathaniel Barlock
Age: 8

CHRISTMAS EVE MORNING

When I am here
I feel as happy as when I get up on Christmas morning.
I see a really nice cat lying on its back.
I hear my dog bark like this, "Woof! Woof! Woof!"
as loud as jumping on a trampoline.
I smell my wet dog after he jumped over the water.

Haley Crawford
Age: 7

A BEAUTIFUL PLACE

When I am here
I feel as relaxed as a person lying on the sand.
I see the flowing water like the ocean.
I hear the sweet sound of birds chirping all around.
I smell the chlorine of a swimming pool.

                                        Melinda Breon
                                        Age: 7

A BEAUTIFUL PLACE TO BE

When I am here
I feel as content as a newborn kitten lying in its bed.
I see birds singing in the meadow out my window.
I hear my cat purring as quiet as my brother
sleeping on my bed.
I smell flowers in my beautiful backyard.

                                        Ashley Stewart
                                        Age: 7

MY PLACE

When I am here
I feel the breeze brushing my cheeks.
I see my dog playing with her toys in the sunlight
I hear my neighbors soaring on the swings.
I smell sweet tree sap in the air.

Joey DeSandre
Age: 7

SMELLS

When I am here
I feel as content as a lamb in the meadow.
I see my puppy trying to eat the grass.
I hear the wind waving the leaves.
I smell the food that my mom is cooking.

Roger Stamm
Age: 7

MY FAVORITE PLACE TO GO

When I am here
I hear the rides whistling.
I see the seeds in the sunflowers.
I see the parade go by like a slow train.
I taste the ice cream as cool as snow.

Taylor Hawbaker
Age: 8

THE HAPPY PLACE TO BE

When I am here
I feel as comfy as a couch.
I see my lamp flickering like lightning.
I hear my dog snorting like a pig.
I smell smoke like fire from our neighbor's chimney.

Lucas Gray
Age: 7

A SPECIAL PLACE IN MY HEART

When I am here
I feel as relaxed as a sleeping dog.
I see my dog Emma in my head.
I hear the sound of the kids playing in the neighborhood.
I smell my dogs that remind me of cookies
fresh from the oven.

Hannah Finton
Age: 7

LISTENING

When I am here
I feel as free as a horse running through a river.
I see my cats chasing a bunny as fast as a tiger.
I hear my cats purring as quiet as a child sleeping.
I smell the fresh fruit ready to be picked.

Isabel Mertick - Sykes
Age: 8

A PLACE I ENJOY TO BE

When I am here
I feel as happy as a rainbow.
I see the fireworks making a flashing sight in the sky.
I hear a big boom like thunder.
I smell fresh coffeecake from the oven.

Alexandra Hughes
Age: 7

MY FAVORITE PLACE

When I am here
I feel a slight breeze on my face
just like when you walk by a fan.
I see the wavy green leaves in the tree
that look like little waves.
I hear the acorns drop off the tree
that looks like an ice-cream cone that's just been dropped.
I smell the crisp wood from the trees.

T. Nathan King
Age: 8

MY FAVORITE PLACE

When I am here
I feel as happy as when I found out
I was going to Disney World.
I see my hermit crab climbing on me
like a champion climber.
I hear a quiet sound of music
coming from my sister's CD player.
I smell a freshly bathed puppy as sweet as a rose.

Tyler Brennan
Age: 8

THE PINE

When I am here
I feel the wind blowing on my face.
I see bluebirds as dark as the ground in their nests.
I hear crickets chirping.
I smell roses as sweet as perfume.

Seth Storll
Age: 7

AT THE DOCK

When I am here
I feel like a new puppy lying in the grass.
I see fish swimming in the water like jets.
I hear splashes in a lake like writing on a paper.
I smell the sweet air.

Cole Harris
Age: 7

IN THE WOODS

When I am here
I feel as happy as a newborn fawn.
I see the birds sailing across the sky.
I hear the leaves circling in the trees.
I smell the pinesap sizzling out of the pine trees.

Andrew Miller
Age: 7

MY HOMETOWN

When I am here . . .
I feel as free as a wild horse in the meadows.
I see the sun looking down at me just like a giraffe.
I hear two birds chirping a happy tune.
I smell the fresh smell of pine trees.

Erik Isola
Age: 8

DEL GROSSO'S

When I am here . . .
I feel as cool as the wind.
I see a bunch of rides like a stampede of horses.
I hear a bunch of bucks coming near me.
I smell a bunch of horses in a haystack in a barn.

Emma Karas
Age: 7

MY MARKET

When I am here . . .
I feel as happy as a clam.
I see houses as big as two elephants.
I hear trucks as loud as two horns.
I smell gas as smelly as a skunk.

Noah Christie
Age: 7

MY WILLOW

When I am here . . .
I feel as happy as a clam.
I see green leaves like the green leprechauns.
I hear birds singing like a choir.
I smell bark like a tray of cookies baking.

Amber Kustaborder
Age: 8

THE PLACE I LOVE

When I am here . . .
I feel as happy as a clam.
I see people splashing like the waves in the sea.
I hear the water splashing
like the waterfalls in the forests.
I smell food like a fresh-baked Pop Tart.

Will Roeshot
Age: 7

HERSHEY

When I am here . . .
I smell fresh air coming and going like a butterfly.
I see hot dogs sizzling on the stands like the hot sun.
I hear people roaring like lions.
I feel as happy as a clam.

Katja Krieger
Age: 7

MY TRIP TO DISNEY WORLD

When I am here . . .
I feel as happy as a clam.
I see a lot of rides like the blueberries
on a blueberry tree.
I hear screaming like a screeching door.
I smell food in the sunlight like the flowers in my garden.

Miranda Myford
Age: 7

MY TRIP TO DISNEY WORLD

When I am here . . .
I feel as happy as an eagle.
I smell fresh dead fish in the sunlight.
I feel the wind blowing on me like an airplane wing.
I hear birds singing like a violin.

Logan Kalmbach
Age: 8

BUFFALO LAND

When I am here . . .
I feel as joyful as a puppy.
I see the horses running across the fields like a storm.
I hear horse hoofs on the ground as loud
as the rumbling of a giant waking.
I smell grass as sweet as candy.

Sarah Rosengrant
Age: 7

MY OLD HOUSE

When I am here . . .
I feel as happy as a clam.
I see my friends playing like puppies.
I hear dogs barking as loud as my cousins.
I smell the air as if I have a candle burning.

Sarah Mosier
Age: 8

MY SCHOOL

When I am here . . .
I feel as happy as a butterfly floating across the sky.
I see kids working as hard as kids
trying to crack a coconut.
I hear kids talking like birds chirping.
I smell pizza like it's right out of Papa John's oven.

Carly Blonski
Age: 8

MY SEA OF DREAMS

When I am here . . .
I feel the bumps of fish against the boat
like kids throwing rocks at my car.
I see a whale's tail splashing on the sand
like a 300,000 pound weight falling in the water.
I hear dolphins splashing like fireworks exploding.
I smell salt water like a soft pretzel with salt.

Jesse William Washell
Age: 7

THE HOUSE

When I am here . . .
I feel happy when I am here in my house.
I see TV's.
I hear dogs barking.
I smell dogs.

Lance Brown
Age: 7

CLOUDS

Clouds, clouds
there are so many
try to count them
clouds, clouds, clouds
they're so white and fluffy
clouds clouds

James Ethan Harper
Age: 10

MY FRIEND KELLY

Kind, short
Blonde hair
A cheerleader
Nice person
Likes animals
Good friend
Neat handwriting

>Harley Brunswick
>Age: 12

SHAOLIN MONK

I once knew a Shaolin Monk,
    Who had a lot of spunk.
He was seven feet tall,
    But his favorite sport was basketball.
He had a pet dragon
    Who sat in his red wagon.
Now he has to go,
    To travel through the snow.

>Andrew Ayers
>Age: 11

SOLDIER

S aved our country
O ur soldiers are brave
L ike the way you fight
D ie with respect
I want to be just like you
E verybody respects you
R ed, white, and blue

>Randi Boyd
>Age: 12

SOLDIER

S ome died
O utstanding sacrifices
L ived through tough times
D o their duty
I n wars
E ntangled in war
R eached new heights

>Cody Currie
>Age: 11

VETERANS DAY

F ree our souls
R eady to defend
E veryone's involved
E ager to help
D id their best
O utstanding performance
M any people died

                                        Jeff Williams
                                            Age: 12

MY DATE

Once I went on a date,
With a boy that was only eight.
He ate like a pig,
And he wore a wig.
He ordered five pies,
And told so many lies.
I had to take him home,
Then I found out he lives in Rome.

                                          Paige Hake
                                            Age: 11

MY CLASSROOM

My classroom is like a circus
The trainer tries to teach the monkeys . . .
They failed!

Katelyn Nellis
Age: 10

BACKPACK

One day I painted my backpack,
My favorite colors, blue and black.
He did a dance, he did a jump,
He jumped onto a camel's hump!
Just as I thought, his colors were fading,
While in the river he was wading.
All the while he sang this song,
"Oh, my colors are so wrong!"

Damara Deal
Age: 11

AUTUMN

The autumn sky
BRUSHING
Over the earth
Like a painting

        The trees
        Glistening
        With color
        After a heavy
        R
         A
          I
           N

The smell
Of freshly cut grass
Fills
The A
    I
   R

        The shadows
        CASTING over the earth
        Like a DARK
                RAIN
                      CLOUD

The breeze
Whips
Through my hair
Taking off the summer heat

        Birdsongs
        Fill my ears
And the autumn days
        Fill my eyes.

Susan T. Rhoades
Age: 13

SCHOOL

I see people.
I hear talking.
I smell fresh pencils.
I taste my lunch.
I feel paper.
I know math.

> Rachel Kerstetter
> Age: 8

CHILDHOOD IS

Childhood is reading GOOD NIGHT MOON.
Then after that, I would fall asleep soon.

Childhood is learning to talk
And, of course, learning to walk.

Childhood is not being able
To see anything on top of the table.

Childhood is hearing my mom and dad say,
"Christina, you grow so much every day."

Childhood is, to me, so much fun!
There will never be a day I'll consider it done.

> Christina Anne Prestine
> Age: 11

CHILDHOOD IS . . .

Spending time with my mom before p.m. kindergarten,
Waiting on a hot day for the Freeze Pops to harden.

Smelling the cookies my mom has just baked,
Tasting my extra-icing birthday cake.

Playing catch with my dad,
Waiting in my room for doing something bad.

Feeling the sand between my toes,
Going to the circus to see the clown's red nose.

Going outside to laugh and play,
Learning something new every day.

                                        Tyler Serres
                                         Age: 11

LEAVING

Everyone is anxious to get out of here.
I can see all the faces around me.
Some are sad.
Others worried.
I can feel all the people around me.
Pushing and waiting.
I can smell all the people.
We haven't had a bath for days.
I can hear all the people,
Shouting,
Crying.
I look at the faces.
Some tear streaked.
Others angry.
Emotions are high.
People are scared,
Angry,
Worried.
I wonder when the bus will arrive.
The air is warm on my skin.
But inside my heart, I am cold.
The storm has been horrible.
Everything is ruined.
Our house is flooded.
Gone are our possessions.
Gone is everything.
I know I probably won't come back.
This place was my home.
I know I will miss it.
I look around again.

My family and I are worried.
I am leaving the place I called home.
I am a refugee from New Orleans.

> Stephani L. Martinelli
> Age: 13

T he turkey I eat
H ouse I live in
A nimals
N orth Star
K yle
F amily
U nited States of America
L ove

> Kyle Reynolds
> Age: 8

BASEBALL

I see the dirt flying in my eyes.
I hear the crowd cheering with excitement.
I smell the fresh hot dogs.
I taste the air when I'm pitching.
I feel the hot sun.
I know I'm at a baseball field.

Morgan Day
Age: 8

DONUTS

Donuts are round.
Donuts are sweet.
Donuts are very good to eat.
Icing, sprinkles, jelly, powder
I scream louder,
"I want more,
Open that bakery door!"

Naomi George
Age: 8

There once was a crab
Who lived in a lab.
He was smart and small,
And had to crawl,
And liked to drive a cab.

> Derek Nolen Heinbaugh
> Age: 10

A POOL

I see water.
I hear water.
I smell chlorine.
I taste water.
I feel water.
I know I'm at a swimming pool.

> Patrick Hadley
> Age: 9

Leaves
Leaves are falling
Leaves are falling slow
Are falling slow, waving through the air
Falling slow, waving through the air, gently.

                                              Sharell Benner
                                                       Age: 9

There once was a man named Bart.
He liked to shop at Kmart.
He would eat wheat,
On the street,
When he went to leave, his car wouldn't start.

                                          Ryan William Foultz
                                                     Age: 10

Saxophone
jazzy, slick
playing, smiling, puffering
woodwind wonder
Musical rose

Jordan Marie Yaukey
Age: 10

DISNEY WORLD

I see Mickey Mouse.
I hear people talking.
I smell lots of tasty food.
I taste my Mickey Mouse waffle.
I feel the water splashing against me.
I know I am at Disney World.

Megan Cornman
Age: 9

There once was a guy named Bob
Who had never liked his job.
One day he quit,
And started to knit,
Then he walked away eating corn on the cob.

Tim Michael Bear
Age: 10

Books are adventures
binded together
teaching children about the world and goals.

Dalida Camdzic
Age: 10

AS LONG AS I HAVE YOU

When summer fades,
and autumn's leaves start turning red,
when wind and rain collide,
and I shiver from the cold in my bed,
I'll think of your arms wrapped around me.
Holding me tight, keeping me close.
You and me, us and we.
That's all I'll think about.

When winter's breeze traps each breath,
and snow starts floating down,
I'll stay by your side to kiss each snowflake off your face,
and lift each and every frown.

When spring's soft fragrance returns to warm our hearts,
and April showers fill days with romance,
we'll take advantage of those times and go out to dance.

When nights surrender to the glow of the moon and stars,
and days become filled with enchanted beams,
you'll be the song of my soul,
the wish of all my dreams.
And all my life will be perfect and true,
as long as I have you.

Dedicated to Daniel Reed

Tiara Mehic
Age: 14

CHILDHOOD IS . . .

Going to the beach and playing in the sand,
Riding the rides at Hershey Park,
Eating sundaes,
Playing board games,
Going to carnivals,
Having picnics,
Going fishing,
Coloring,
Learning to swim,
And baking cookies.

Taylor Marie Fromm
Age: 12

He hits a homer!
It soars into crowded stands.
The crowd cheers him on!

David Mitchell
Age: 10

WOODS

I see the squirrels running up the tree.
I hear the leaves crackle under my feet.
I smell the leaves.
I taste the air.
I feel the tree bark.
I know I'm in the woods!

>Kelsi Minich
>Age: 8

I like karate.
You get to punch, kick, and scream.
But take a breather.

>Taylor Wickard
>Age: 10

NO TUTU FOR LULU!

There once was a dog named Lulu,
Who had dreamed of having a tutu!
So she went to the store,
It was tutus galore,
But she had no money. Boohoo!

Andrea Taylor Adolph
Age: 11

CHILDHOOD IS . . .

Going to the beach a lot,
When it is very hot.

Playing in the waves,
Not having to work like a slave.

Riding waves at Hershey Park
Is lots of fun in the dark!

Always playing in the pool,
Would always keep me very cool!

I always went to the mall.
Everyone looked so tall.

Sarah Telep
Age: 11

Leaves are colorful
On those beautiful bark trees.
I watch them fall down.

Carissa Brandt
Age: 10

Athletes are awesome!
Love competitions a lot!
Gatorade stops sweat.

Jake Khoussine
Age: 10

Lollipops
good, round
eating, sucking, licking
yummy in tummy
Red plate

                                  Lindsay R. Bower
                                  Age: 10

Snow, snow it is here
White floating snow falling down
Pretty fluffy snow

                                  Laura Renee Ryan
                                  Age: 11

SHE'LL BE THERE

Memory of my mom:

At the mall
   She'll be there
At college
   She'll be there
At my wedding
   She'll be there
When I have my first child!
   She'll be there
Through stumps and falls
   She'll be there
Through those tears
   She'll be there
In your heart she'll stay.

Remember
        loved
                ones.

                                      Taya Sky Erway

CHRISTMAS TREE

White
With lights
It sparkles
In the moonlight
With a train
Wrapped around tight
Green balls
White balls
Red
Hanging in the window
Just for show
Luminously bright
The stars fight
At night
To see the pretty
White light
Of the star
On
  Just
    Right

                        Emily A. Sweeney
                        Age: 10

CHRISTMAS PRESENTS

candy in full jars
playing with toy cars
presents under the tree all just for me
sharing caring lots of fun
all day long 'til the day's done

Nathan Adam Whitney
Age: 8

A CRAZY DAY

The horses all ran courses.
The cats all ate rats.
The dogs all played in the fog.
The sheep all heard loud beeps.
The cows all took their bows.
The pigs all wore wigs.
The deer all could hear clear.

What a crazy day to be here!

Paisha Glisson
Age: 8

SWIRLING

         It starts in the middle
      and   works
    its way   out swirling,   curling,
    twirling   about. Will this   madness
    ever end?   Because   all the   sides just
    bend.   Nothing can   stop   it, it just
    continues   on, but who   is to   say for
    how long.   As long   as the   words
    keep flowing,   the swirl
    continues   growing.
      But when the swirl no longer
       bends, that is when the
           swirl will end!

Lisa A. Miller
Age: 16

I'M SORRY

I wish I could see your face
I wish people would give me some space,
So I could deal with all the pain
Of never seeing you again.
I know we weren't very close
And that is one thing I will miss the most.
I thought you'd be around for a while
And I would continue to see your innocent smile.
But now it's gone, and that's too bad;
I'll never see or talk to you, which makes me sad.
I wish I had gotten to know you better
But now I'm writing you this letter,
Hoping you'll see it from up above
And shower down your compassion and love.
"Good-bye. I'm sorry," it will say.
I'll never forget you until my dying day.

Emily Degnitz
Age: 17

THE PEOPLE IN MY HEART

Two people have changed my life forever.
They're like sunshine on a dark and rainy day.
They're the yellows in your life
when all you can see is gray.
They're like a sparkling flower in a pile of weeds.
They're happiness when sad is the only thing you feel.
When I'm mad and wonder why I keep going on,
I remember the two people that make my life worthwhile.
These people have been with me every step of the way.
They make me smile and laugh.
These two people mean the world to me.
They are my Nan and Pap.
The two people in my heart.

Kaitlyn Mihajlov
Age: 13

Shallow hearts keep the beat along the false path,
   Leading you to the ever-going lies.

Souls will be torn apart by this evil,
   Love will never again be full of the bliss.

Falling into a pit of hatred,
   From which you will never emerge.

Unwanted and unseen to all those that seem to matter,
   You will be unable to make their expectations.

THIS IS MY "NORMAL" LIFE.

Rebekah Molnar
Age: 13

BILLY

In the silence, one child speaks
But no one bothers to listen
In a crowded hallway one child cries
But no one sees his tears glisten

He sits alone without a friend
His silence will never end
He hopes just one person will see
How talkative and fun he can be

Day after day no one comes nearby
And the little boy just sits and cries
He lost his hope and bliss
Did it have to come down to this?

Monday morning rolls around
The children study, there is no sound
And in the silence one child speaks
"Why isn't Billy here?"

Christine McCarl
Age: 15